A Note from
Mary Pope Osborne About the

MAGIC TREE HOUSE®
FACT TRACKERS

When I write Magic Tree House® adventures, I love including facts about the times and places Jack and Annie visit. But when readers finish these adventures, I want them to learn even more. So that's why we write a series of nonfiction books that are companions to the fiction titles in the Magic Tree House® series. We call these books Fact Trackers because we love to track the facts! Whether we're researching dinosaurs, pyramids, Pilgrims, sea monsters, or cobras, we're always amazed at how wondrous and surprising the real world is. We want you to experience the same wonder we do—so get out your pencils and notebooks and hit the trail with us. You can be a Magic Tree House® Fact Tracker, too!

Mary Pope Osborne

Here's what kids, parents, and teachers have to say about the Magic Tree House® Fact Trackers:

"They are so good. I can't wait for the next one. All I can say for now is prepare to be amazed!" —Alexander N.

"I have read every Magic Tree House book there is. The [Fact Trackers] are a thrilling way to get more information about the special events in the story." —John R.

"These are fascinating nonfiction books that enhance the magical time-traveling adventures of Jack and Annie. I love these books, especially *American Revolution.* I was learning so much, and I didn't even know it!" —Tori Beth S.

"[They] are an excellent 'behind-the-scenes' look at what the [Magic Tree House fiction] has started in your imagination! You can't buy one without the other; they are such a complement to one another." —Erika N., mom

"Magic Tree House [Fact Trackers] took my children on a journey from Frog Creek, Pennsylvania, to so many significant historical events! The detailed manuals are a remarkable addition to the classic fiction Magic Tree House books we adore!" —Jenny S., mom

"[They] are very useful tools in my classroom, as they allow for students to be part of the planning process. Together, we find facts in the [Fact Trackers] to extend the learning introduced in the fictional companions. Researching and planning classroom activities, such as our class Olympics based on facts found in *Ancient Greece and the Olympics,* help create a genuine love for learning!" —Paula H., teacher

MAGIC TREE HOUSE®
FACT TRACKER

Leonardo da Vinci

A NONFICTION COMPANION TO MAGIC TREE HOUSE MERLIN MISSION #10:
Monday with a Mad Genius

BY MARY POPE OSBORNE
AND NATALIE POPE BOYCE

ILLUSTRATED BY SAL MURDOCCA

A STEPPING STONE BOOK™
Random House 🏠 New York

The Magic Tree House Fact Tracker series was formerly known as the
Magic Tree House Research Guide series. Magic Tree House Merlin Mission
#10 was formerly known as Magic Tree House #38.

Visit us on the Web!
SteppingStonesBooks.com
MagicTreeHouse.com

Educators and librarians, for a variety of teaching tools, visit us at
RHTeachersLibrarians.com

Library of Congress Cataloging-in-Publication Data
Osborne, Mary Pope.
Leonardo da Vinci : a nonfiction companion to Magic Tree House #38 : Monday
with a mad genius / by Mary Pope Osborne and Natalie Pope Boyce ;
illustrated by Sal Murdocca.
 p. cm. — (Magic tree house fact tracker)
"Originally published by Random House Children's Books, New York, in 2009"
"A Stepping Stone book."
Includes index.
ISBN 978-0-375-84665-6 (trade) — ISBN 978-0-375-94665-3 (lib. bdg.) —
ISBN 978-0-307-97549-2 (ebook)
1. Leonardo, da Vinci, 1452–1519—Juvenile literature. 2. Artists—Italy—
Biography—Juvenile literature. I. Leonardo, da Vinci, 1452–1519. II. Boyce,
Natalie Pope. III. Murdocca, Sal. IV. Osborne, Mary Pope. Monday with a
mad genius. V. Title.
N6923.L33 O82 2011 709.2—dc22 [B] 2011006596

Printed in the United States of America
27 26 25 24

This book has been officially leveled by using the F&P Text Level Gradient™
Leveling System.

For Liza Fosburgh

Scientific Consultant:
EDWARD RODLEY, Exhibit Coordinator, Museum of Science, Boston

Art History Consultant:
STEPHEN CAMPBELL, Chair, Department of the History of Art, Johns Hopkins University

Education Consultant:
HEIDI JOHNSON, Earth Science and Paleontology, Lowell Junior High School, Bisbee, Arizona

Very special thanks to Virginia Berbrich for her photographs, and to the terrific team at Random House: Gloria Cheng, Mallory Loehr, Lisa Findlay, and especially Diane Landolf.

LEONARDO DA VINCI

Contents

Dear Readers,

When we got back from our adventure in <u>Monday with a Mad Genius</u>, we thought we knew all about Leonardo da Vinci. But then we started fact-tracking!

We found out it would take a roomful of books to tell you everything about this amazing man. Leonardo was an incredible artist, inventor, and scientist. He put a lot of ideas down in notebooks that still exist today. He also drew plans for paintings and sculptures in them. Leonardo's notebooks can be hard to read: he wrote his letters backward! (You can find out why in this book.)

To be fact trackers, we started at the

library. We tracked down lots of books about Leonardo. There were great pictures in a lot of them. You can see what he wrote and drew in his notebooks and look at his beautiful paintings. We also tracked facts on the Internet. But not all the websites about Leonardo are good ones. Always have your teachers or parents check out the information you're getting online. Then be like Leonardo and fill up notebooks with your findings.

We can hardly wait for you to meet this amazing genius!

Jack
Annie

1

Leonardo da Vinci and His World

Leonardo da Vinci was one of the greatest artists and thinkers the world has ever known. He was also an incredible scientist and inventor. Although Leonardo lived over five hundred years ago, we still admire his genius today.

Leonardo was born on April 15, 1452, in a village in central Italy called Vinci. Leonardo's name means "Leonardo from

Vinci." Leonardo's grandfather wrote the date of his grandson's birth in a notebook. This notebook still exists in a library in Italy.

Unfortunately, we do not know much about Leonardo's childhood. There are stories that he liked to draw. We can guess that he drew plants and animals he saw in the countryside around Vinci. And we also know that he loved music. He learned to play a stringed instrument called a lyre.

Leonardo began keeping notebooks and journals when he was thirty.

Leonardo's Notebooks

There are some famous stories about Leonardo from people who knew him or knew about him. We also have many of his notebooks and journals to study. They give us a good idea of how Leonardo's mind worked.

Leonardo usually carried a notebook with him. When he went out, he attached it

Around twenty-five notebooks with over 7,000 pages survive today.

to his belt. Leonardo said that an artist must always be ready to make a sketch. "Look around," he said. "Watch people carefully."

Leonardo used his notebooks to make notes and sketches for his inventions and art. He also wrote down things that interested him or things that he researched. After his death, many of the notebooks were lost. Some remaining notebooks are really copies by people who lived after Leonardo.

A famous art expert once said that Leonardo da Vinci was the most curious person in history. His notebooks show that he wondered about everything. He even thought about small things—like the way a woodpecker's tongue worked or how a person sneezed.

Baby Leonardo and the Kite

Leonardo wrote that his first memory was when he was a baby lying in his cradle. He said that a bird called a *kite* swooped down on him, brushing its tail between his lips.

 A <u>kite</u> is a bird in the same family as hawks and eagles.

Leonardo didn't seem sure whether this was a dream or whether it really happened. But he claimed that it was why he became interested in birds. All of his life, Leonardo drew pictures of birds, especially of their wings. He tried to figure out how the wings worked so he could build a flying machine. He thought that one day people might be able to fly—just like birds.

The Renaissance

Leonardo lived during a time called the *Renaissance* (REH-nuh-sahns). The Renaissance began in the 1300s and lasted about 300 years. It started in Italy and spread to the rest of Europe.

Renaissance comes from a French word meaning "rebirth."

During the Renaissance, people took a fresh look at the ideas and art of ancient Greece and Rome. They rediscovered Greek and Roman art and architecture. They read Greek and Roman writers. All these things made people excited about science, art, music, and books. Great

universities, hospitals, and libraries sprang up across Europe.

The Ospedale degli Innocenti, or Foundling Hospital, in Florence shows the ancient Greek and Roman influence on architecture.

The Renaissance was also a time when architects made grand buildings. Lots of them looked like buildings found in ancient Greece and Rome.

Patrons

Many rich and powerful people had an interest in the arts. They often hired the best artists, poets, musicians, and craftsmen to work for them. These wealthy people were called *patrons*.

Sometimes artists lived and worked with the same patrons for years. An artist was lucky to get a rich patron. It meant he could earn a living with steady work.

Florence

Vinci was not far from the city of Florence. Florence was the center of Renaissance

Lorenzo de Medici was a rich patron of the arts in Florence.

thinking in Italy. When Leonardo was a teenager, he moved to Florence with his family. It was the perfect place for a young genius like Leonardo.

Mirror Writing

Leonardo often wrote in a strange handwriting called *mirror writing*. He wrote from right to left, not left to right. He also wrote his letters backward. If you hold a page of Leonardo's writing up to a mirror, it looks like regular writing.

Experts say that Leonardo wrote like this because he was left-handed and wrote with ink. In Leonardo's day, ink took a long time to dry. The ink would smear as a person dragged his left hand across the page. When Leonardo wrote things for other people to read, he wrote normally.

2

Leonardo in Florence

During the Renaissance, Italy was not a united country. Powerful cities set up their own governments and made their own laws. Sometimes the cities even fought one another.

Florence was famous for its wool and silk trade and for its great banking houses. When Leonardo arrived, over fifty thousand people lived there. There were more than a hundred churches and fifty public squares.

Seven miles of walls surrounded the town.

Great families like the Medicis built huge houses called *palazzi* (puh-LOT-see). They hired skilled people to fill their palazzi with fine furniture and art.

 This Medici house had beautiful paintings on the wall and on the ceilings, too!

The most important church in any city was called the <u>cathedral</u>.

A very beautiful *cathedral* (kuh-THEE-druhl) called the *Duomo* towered over the city. Its shining red dome reached 370 feet into the sky. People could see it from miles away. Whenever someone who lived in Florence left the city, they said they were cathedral-sick instead of homesick.

The Heart of the City

The market was the heart of the city. It was in a large stone square in the oldest part of town. Since ancient times, people had gathered there to buy and sell things. The market was alive with sights, sounds, and smells. Merchants called out their wares. Men on horseback rode through the crowd announcing the news of the day. People shouted and laughed as they argued over prices and greeted their friends.

The smells of flowers, spices, bread, and other food filled the air. Thousands of people crowded together to buy cloth, cooking utensils, and food of all kinds.

Leonardo loved animals and was a vegetarian for most of his life. There is a story that he often bought caged birds in the market. He would hold them in his hand for a moment and then set them free.

Leonardo drew cats in all kinds of poses.

At Home

Most people lived above shops lining the busy city streets. Sometimes whole families crowded into one room. The rooms were often dark and cramped.

People did not have much furniture. Instead of glass, oil paper covered the windows. Some of the older buildings did not have chimneys. Smoke escaped through a hole in the roof.

Guilds

Craftsmen, artists, and merchants of all kinds belonged to groups called *guilds*. Guilds were made up of people who were in the same kind of trade. Each guild set up rules that were followed by everyone in the trade. Guild members had busy workshops all over the city.

There were over twenty different guilds in Florence.

There were guilds for wool and silk workers, woodworkers, bankers, and even cheese sellers and butchers.

Pharmacists also mixed and sold medicine.

Artists did not have their own guild. They belonged to the guild of doctors and pharmacists (FAR-muh-sists). Artists bought powders for making paint from the pharmacists.

Leonardo the Apprentice

Leonardo had been drawing since he was a child. His father knew that his son was very gifted. He took some of Leonardo's drawings to a famous artist named Verrocchio. Verrocchio agreed to take Leonardo as his *apprentice* (uh-PREN-tiss).

An <u>apprentice</u> works for a skilled person in order to learn a trade.

Apprentices often began working when they were fourteen. Experts think

34

Leonardo was about sixteen when he joined Verrocchio.

In Verrocchio's busy workshop, Leonardo and the other boys learned how to work with silver, marble, bronze, and wood. The boys even learned to make bells and musical instruments. It was also their job to keep the workshop clean and to do other chores, such as mixing paint and cleaning brushes.

No fair! Girls could not be apprentices!

Pigment is dried powder in different colors made from plants or minerals.

Verrocchio taught Leonardo to paint. At that time, most artists painted with *tempera*. Tempera is made of colors, or *pigments*, that are mixed with egg yolks. Verrocchio showed Leonardo how to use oil paints, which was a new way of painting.

In oil painting, pigments are mixed with oil instead of eggs. Oil paintings take a long time to dry. The colors are deep and rich and blend together well.

Leonardo's First Painting

When apprentices were skilled enough, they worked on paintings with their masters. Many experts believe that Leonardo painted an angel and the background in Verrocchio's painting *The Baptism of Christ.*

There is a story that when Verrocchio

saw Leonardo's work, he realized that his student was a better artist than he was. It is said that Verrocchio vowed never to paint again.

The Baptism of Christ

Leonardo's angel

Leonardo's Workshop

When Leonardo was twenty years old, he left Verrocchio's service to go out on his own. Leonardo joined a guild and set up a workshop. He started to paint and sculpt. He soon had a reputation as a great artist and began to get requests for work.

Leonardo drew this portrait of a warrior when he was a young man in Florence.

Leonardo's life in Florence was busy. He was handsome and popular and loved to cook for his friends. People used to laugh at his riddles and jokes. Leonardo kept a large lizard in his studio that he dressed in fake horns and wings to scare his visitors.

Duke Sforza and Milan

After ten years on his own, Leonardo needed a powerful patron. He wrote a letter to Duke Sforza, the ruler of Milan, to ask for a job in his court. Leonardo wrote that he had skills as an inventor and engineer as well as an artist. His letter worked. The duke hired him, and Leonardo left Florence for Milan.

Leonardo stayed in Milan for seventeen years. He did some of his best work there. But Leonardo never forgot Florence. In the years ahead, he would go back many times.

Leonardo the Musician

Leonardo also played music for Duke Sforza. He took a lyre to Milan that he had designed himself. It was made of silver and shaped like a horse's head. The kind of lyre Leonardo played had seven strings. It looked a little like an upside-down violin. It was played with a bow.

There are stories that when Leonardo played his lyre, he sang poems and was good at making up words on the spot. There is also evidence that Leonardo wrote music, but none of his music exists today.

41

3

Leonardo the Dreamer

In his letter to the duke, Leonardo said he could create bridges that were light and strong. He also claimed he knew how to drain water from ditches, build cannons, protect warships, destroy forts, and even build armored cars!

Leonardo drew and wrote down hundreds of ideas for inventions and experiments in his notebooks. Most of his designs were never built. People did not have the

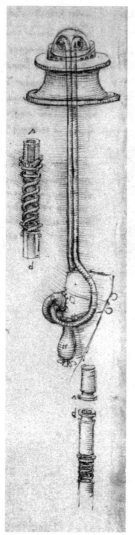

skills, tools, or money needed to build them. In Leonardo's day, electricity had not yet been discovered. The power to operate machines came from people or animals.

Leonardo planned big projects like flying machines, canals, buildings, and bridges. He even designed his idea of the perfect city. But Leonardo also thought up smaller things, such as contact lenses, shoes for walking on water, diving suits, life preservers, and webbed swimming gloves.

Leonardo made this sketch of an underwater breathing device.

Most people had never thought of these things before. Leonardo was a dreamer who was way ahead of his time. He imagined how things could work. Then he put his dreams down on paper.

Armored Cars

Leonardo told the duke that he could make an armored car so strong that no weapon could pierce it. Leonardo's plans for the armored car looked a lot like a modern tank.

This shows Leonardo's sketch of an armored car alongside a modern tank.

Even though Leonardo created war machines, he actually hated war. He called it a "beastly madness."

Leonardo planned for eight men inside the tank to turn cranks connected to the wheels. There would be holes in the sides so the soldiers could fire weapons.

For a while, Leonardo thought that horses could be used to turn the cranks. Later, he decided they might get too scared.

If Leonardo's tank had been built, it would have been too heavy to operate. And the wheels would have turned in opposite directions!

Today tanks are common in the army. But tanks weren't built until 1912— almost 400 years after Leonardo's death.

Boats and Submarines

Leonardo designed a boat with two layers covering the bottom. Today we call

46

this a double-hulled boat. If a cannonball or another object went through the first layer, the second would keep water from pouring in and sinking the boat. Leonardo's idea was a good one. In fact, it's an idea that we use today. For safety reasons, all modern passenger ships must have double hulls.

Leonardo also drew up plans for a one-man submarine. It could not go all the way underwater. Leonardo's sub was supposed to sneak up on other ships and ram into them.

It wasn't until the twentieth century that submarines were commonly used in sea battles. Today subs go completely underwater and stay down for days. In 1940, the Italians named one of their submarines the *Leonardo da Vinci* in honor of the great inventor.

This is a model based on Leonardo's design for a paddle boat.

Leonardo also designed a giant slingshot and a triple-barreled cannon.

Weapons of War

Leonardo designed lots of different weapons for the duke. He invented a cannon that could shoot cannonballs over 10,000

48

feet! He also spent time planning new types of crossbows.

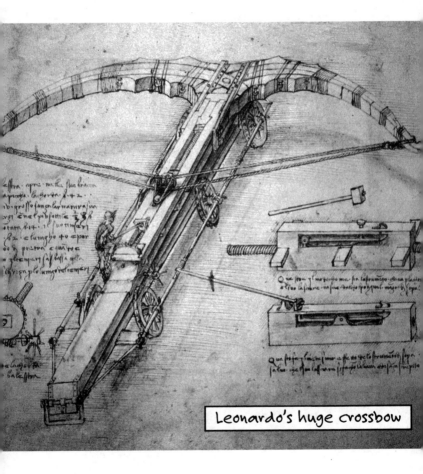

Leonardo's huge crossbow

Crossbows were weapons that shot arrows called bolts. In Leonardo's day, soldiers often used three-man crossbows. They could hit targets over 400 yards away.

Leonardo had plans for a huge crossbow that was never built. It was a one-man crossbow the size of an eighteen-wheeler!

Leonardo had many ideas for other weapons—he designed multi-barreled machine guns, missiles, and grenades.

Leonardo's Parachute

Leonardo invented a cloth parachute. It was made of linen and weighed over eighty-seven pounds. He claimed that his parachute would protect someone who jumped from any height.

In 2000, a skydiver named Adrian Nicholas decided to test Leonardo's claim.

He built a parachute just like Leonardo's
drawing. Adrian put the parachute on. Then

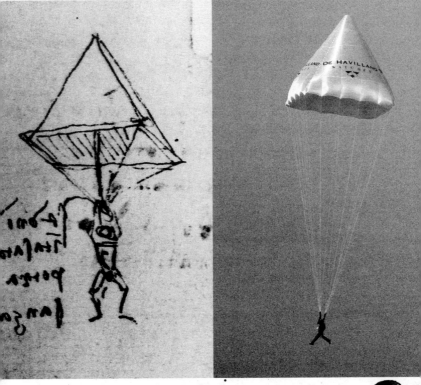

Adrian Nicholas made his parachute
based on this Leonardo sketch.

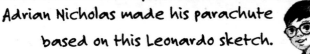

he jumped out of a hot-air balloon that was 10,000 feet above the ground! And guess what? Leonardo got it right! Adrian landed safely. Whew!

The Beautiful Bridge

In 1502, Sultan Bayezid II of Turkey hired Leonardo to design a special bridge for him. Leonardo drew up beautiful plans. Unfortunately, the sultan decided he could not build the bridge.

But five hundred years later, a Norwegian engineer used Leonardo's design. He

The bridge in Aas, Norway, is for foot traffic, not cars or trucks.

built an incredible bridge in southern Norway. He called his plan the Leonardo da Vinci Bridge Project.

Leonardo's Flying Machines

Leonardo designed lots of different flying machines. One type was called an *ornithopter.*

Leonardo planned for a pilot to lie on a wooden platform under the wings. The pilot would use his feet to push pedals hooked up to the bottom of the wings. Leonardo hoped that this would give the plane enough power to rise up off the ground.

Ornithopter comes from the Greek roots ornitho, which means "bird," and ter, which means "wing."

But Leonardo seemed a little worried about his plan. He wrote that it would be a good idea to fly over a lake. He advised the pilot to tie a flotation device around his waist in case he fell in.

There were also plans for gliders and two-man ornithopters, with each pilot operating one wing.

Leonardo also sketched plans for a helicopter. He meant for a large screw to be turned fast enough to lift it off the ground.

Leonardo's helicopter looks a lot different from a modern one.

Did Leonardo Ever Fly?

No one knows if Leonardo ever built a flying machine. But people are curious about something he wrote in his journal:

The great bird will take its first flight from Mount Ceceri, which will fill the world with amazement.

Mount Ceceri was near Leonardo's home. Was the great bird a flying machine? Did Leonardo himself try to fly?

There are stories that he tried and failed. There is also a well-known story that one of his apprentices tried but crash-landed and broke his leg. If this is true, Leonardo probably did not give up. He always had big dreams.

Leonardo said that if people could ever fly, it would be so wonderful that they would walk around all day looking up at the sky. Leonardo would be happy with our world today. Whenever people travel on airplanes, they soar among the clouds . . . just like birds.

The Black Death

While Leonardo lived in Milan, a terrible disease spread through the city, killing thousands of people. Its victims got black spots all over their bodies before they died. People named the disease the *black death*. Today we call it the *bubonic plague*. At one time, the plague wiped out about a third of the people in Europe.

In Renaissance cities like Milan, sewage ran in the streets. Rats and their fleas were everywhere. Infected fleas bit people and infected them as well.

Leonardo knew that Milan was not healthy. So he planned a special city, where people could live better and cleaner lives.

In Italy in the 1600s, doctors wore beaked masks stuffed with herbs they thought would protect them from the plague. We're not sure if the masks were used in Leonardo's time.

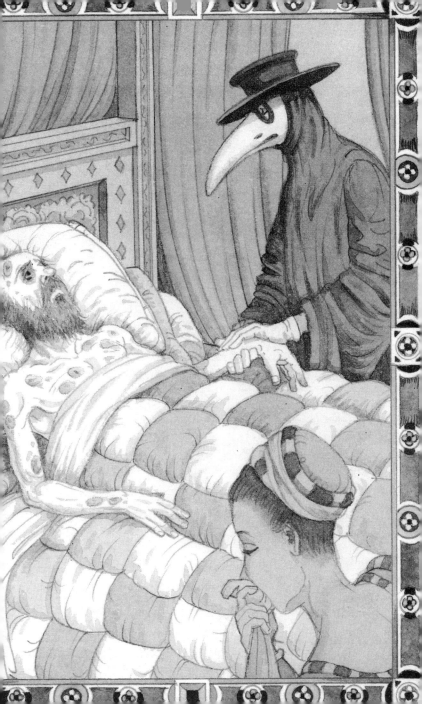

4

Leonardo the Scientist

Leonardo wondered about everything. He examined rocks and fossils to learn what the world was like long ago. He studied the way water moved and how water pressure could be used to power machines.

Leonardo also recorded storms and studied the weather. He wrote about the way a whirlwind ripped roofs off buildings. He studied clouds and lightning and rain. He even figured out that the moon had an effect on the tides.

Leonardo and the Human Body

Leonardo was really curious about how the human body worked. He wanted to know everything about the eyes, the skeleton, and the muscles. He wondered how blood pumped through the body. Leonardo studied human *anatomy* throughout his life. There were no X-ray machines to see inside the human body during Leonardo's time.

Anatomy is the shape and makeup of animals and plants.

Leonardo attended lectures on anatomy at universities and hospitals. His teachers often *dissected* human bodies during class. Leonardo drew pictures of what he saw at the dissections.

To dissect is to cut apart any piece of a plant or dead animal in order to study it.

Later, Leonardo did his own dissections. Back then, it was against the law to dissect a human body without special permission. As an artist, Leonardo managed to get this permission. He dissected thirty bodies of all types, young and old.

First, Leonardo studied the muscles

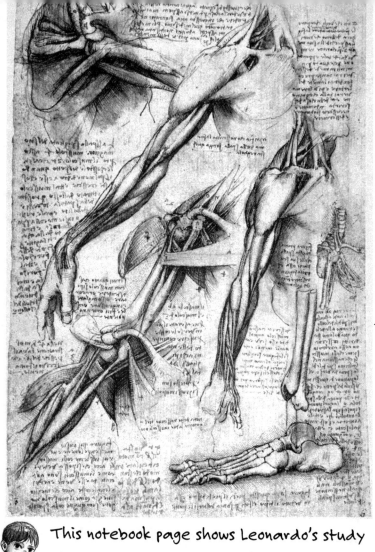

This notebook page shows Leonardo's study of the shoulder, arm, and foot.

and tendons. Later, he drew the skeleton, heart, and blood vessels. These drawings are amazingly detailed. Leonardo planned to use them in a book about human anatomy.

Leonardo gave us some rules for healthy living:

Leonardo's Rules for Good Health

Do not eat unless you are hungry.
Eat simple, well-cooked food.
Watch out for anger and stuffy air.
Chew well.
Stay covered up at night.
Rest and keep your mind cheerful.

Leonardo the Botanist

Leonardo often studied nature. He became a good *botanist*. A botanist is someone who knows all about plants. Leonardo made wonderful drawings of flowers, trees,

This is one of Leonardo's beautiful flower drawings.

leaves, and even stalks of grain. His drawings show every detail of the plant. Sometimes Leonardo sketched a plant from several different angles. Sadly, only thirteen of his beautiful plant studies remain.

Fossils

Leonardo knew that mountains in northern Italy had layers of shells and fossils. Most people believed a great flood had once covered the mountains. They thought when the flood went down, it left behind the fossils and shells.

Leonardo did not think this was true. He thought it would be impossible for a flood to leave fossils and shells in separate layers. He also concluded that after the flood was over, the water would have washed the fossils downhill, off the mountain.

Leonardo thought that before the mountains existed, a great sea covered the land. Fossils and shells were deposited in layers on the ocean floor. When the mountains formed, they pushed the fossils and shells up with them. Today scientists say that Leonardo was absolutely right.

Leonardo studied fossils of ancient sea creatures like this one.

"Open your eyes!" he said. All his life, Leonardo opened his eyes to the natural world. And he never stopped thinking about why things happened the way they did.

Turn the page to find out what Leonardo looked like.

What Did Leonardo Look Like?

No one is certain how Leonardo really looked. But experts think Leonardo used himself as a model for the first two drawings shown here. They also think that the artist Raphael used Leonardo as a model for Plato in his painting of Greek philosophers, called *The School of Athens*.

Probably a self-portrait

The Vitruvian Man

The School of Athens

Plato

5

Leonardo the Artist

When Leonardo wrote to Duke Sforza, he said, "In painting, I can do everything that it is possible to do." Leonardo was a master at showing the way clothes drape over the body and the colors and details of skin and hair. His paintings have deep, rich colors.

Leonardo worked on new ways to paint, so that things in the front of the painting looked closer than those in the background. He also used light and dark paints to make the paintings seem more natural.

Studio in Milan

Leonardo said a studio should be a place with flowers, music, and order.

Leonardo wrote a book for his students about how to paint and draw.

Like Verrocchio, Leonardo had apprentices. He was said to be a strict teacher. He would not allow his apprentices to paint until they were twenty years old. They had to learn to draw first.

One of Leonardo's favorite apprentices was nicknamed Salai. He came to the studio when he was ten. Even though Leonardo was fond of him, Salai was very naughty. In fact, his nickname means "little devil." Leonardo often caught Salai

stealing things. Salai hoped to sell the stolen items to buy candy.

Salai stayed with Leonardo for many years. When Leonardo died, he left Salai a small garden, a house, and some famous paintings.

The Giant Horse

Verrocchio had taught Leonardo how to cast bronze statues. One day, Duke Sforza asked Leonardo to design a huge bronze horse. It was to be the biggest horse statue in all of Italy. The duke wanted the statue to honor his father.

This is one of many sketches for the Sforza monument.

Leonardo studied other horse statues. He drew horses in different poses. At first, Leonardo planned to show the horse rearing up on its hind legs.

But he realized this was impossible. Too much weight would be on the hind legs. Finally Leonardo and his apprentices built a clay model of a prancing horse. It was sixteen feet tall and twenty-four feet long from nose to tail. Leonardo's great horse was three times bigger than a real horse. People cheered when Leonardo and the apprentices placed the clay statue in front of the duke's palace at last.

Twenty-four feet is about as long as four tall men.

Leonardo was making plans to cast the statue in bronze. At the same time, the French invaded Milan. The duke had to use the bronze intended for the horse to make cannons.

The duke had set aside forty tons of bronze for the statue.

When the soldiers arrived, they used the clay statue for target practice. Leonardo's great horse was destroyed.

The Last Supper

Leonardo was hired to do a painting on the wall of a church. It was to be a picture of the last meal that Jesus had with his *disciples* (dih-SY-puhlz). This painting is called *The Last Supper.*

Disciples are people who follow a master and spread his teachings.

After Leonardo drew many studies, he and his apprentices began the painting. They painted the wall with tempera and oils.

An eyewitness said that Leonardo often arrived early and got right to work. Sometimes he worked all day without stopping. Other times, he stayed away for several days to work on the horse.

Leonardo often stood with his arms folded, studying the painting. Once he raced into the church, scrambled up the ladder, painted one or two quick strokes, and left.

The painting shows Jesus sitting at the center of the table. His twelve disciples are on either side. The colors are soft, and their faces are full of emotion.

Leonardo looked around Milan to find the perfect faces to use as models for Jesus and the disciples.

There was one big problem. The method Leonardo used to seal the wall did not work. The church was damp. Soon the paint began to flake and fade.

Over the years, there has been a lot of damage to *The Last Supper*. The room has flooded several times. Once, the church was used as a stable. A door was cut into the middle of the painting. The closest call came during World War II, when bombs exploded nearby and cracked the walls.

Experts have tried hard to restore *The Last Supper*. The last restoration took twenty years. Many people say the new

colors are too bright and the faces look different. Sadly, we will never see Leonardo's work the way it was.

Leonardo spent three years on <u>The Last Supper</u>. This is a copy of the original painting.

Mona Lisa

The *Mona Lisa* may be the most famous painting in the world. Experts say Mona Lisa was a young woman married to a rich man. Many believe her husband hired Leonardo to make a painting of her.

Leonardo began the *Mona Lisa* in 1503. He worked on it for about three years. For reasons we're not sure of, Leonardo kept the painting. He still had it with him when he died sixteen years later.

People wonder if Mona Lisa is smiling. And if she is smiling, what is she smiling at?

To create this feeling of mystery, Leonardo painted tiny strokes of color around Mona Lisa's eyes and mouth. Experts say there are over forty layers

There is a story that Leonardo hired singers and musicians to keep Mona Lisa happy while he painted.

Mona Lisa's last name was Gioconda. Sometimes the painting is called <u>La Gioconda</u>.

of color. This *technique* (tek-NEEK) is called *sfumato* (sfoo-MAH-toe). Leonardo invented it.

A <u>technique</u> is a way of doing something.

83

The word *sfumato* means "smoked" or "smoky" in Italian. Sfumato blurs colors together. It creates a smoky effect and softens the lines between objects. Sfumato makes it hard to tell if Mona Lisa is smiling or if there are shadows around her mouth.

When Leonardo died, he gave the *Mona Lisa* to Salai. Later, the king of France bought it. Today it is in the Louvre (LOOV) Museum in Paris.

Battle of Anghiari

The city of Florence hired Leonardo to paint a scene showing a famous battle between the armies of Milan and Florence. The painting would be known as the *Battle of Anghiari*. Leonardo was to paint it on a wall at the Palazzo Vecchio.

The Palazzo Vecchio was the town hall.

For two years, Leonardo drew battle scenes in his notebooks. They show horses and men tangled together in fierce combat. The sketches are powerful and brutal. They are reminders of the horrors of war. Some experts think they are Leonardo's best work.

Leonardo used wax to bind the paint to the wall. As he began to paint, a terrible rainstorm hit Florence. Water poured down the walls. The storm continued all night.

Leonardo put heating pots all around the room to dry out the walls. But the heat melted the wax. The painting was badly damaged, and Leonardo had only finished a small part of it. We do not know why, but Leonardo never tried to paint it again.

Years later, someone painted over the wall. Today all that we know of the painting is from Leonardo's great drawings.

Mona Lisa Stolen!

On August 21, 1911, Paris was in an uproar. The *Mona Lisa* was missing! Someone had taken it right off the wall at the Louvre.

Sixty detectives and a hundred policemen all rushed to the museum. The Louvre closed for a week while they searched for clues.

Police questioned the guard who was supposed to be watching the painting. He confessed he'd gone outside for five minutes to smoke a cigarette.

In spite of constant police work, the painting could not be found. Everyone feared the *Mona Lisa* was lost forever.

Two years later, the painting turned up

in Florence when the thief tried to sell it.
Since that time, the *Mona Lisa* has been
guarded night and day. It is now protected
within a very strong glass case.

6

People in Leonardo's World

Leonardo knew some of the most famous people of his day. Not all of them were artists. Some were mathematicians, architects, musicians, statesmen, philosophers, and poets. All of them had the spirit of the Renaissance. They were excited by new ideas and discoveries.

Leonardo wrote that people should always be eager to hear the opinions of others.

He and his friends often got together to talk and exchange ideas.

When Leonardo was in Milan, he met Luca Pacioli. Luca was a famous mathematician who wrote books about math. He also taught at the university. Leonardo became interested in math and asked Luca to be his teacher. They became such good friends that Luca moved in with him. Both men fled Milan when the French attacked the city.

Isabelle d'Este was another one of Leonardo's friends. Isabelle was a wealthy woman from a royal family. Unlike many other women of her time, she'd had an excellent education. Isabelle became a true Renaissance woman who loved to learn. She was interested in the arts and was a patron for several painters. Like Leonardo, she was also an inventor and a good musician.

Leonardo did a drawing of her that still exists today.

Perhaps the friend Leonardo owed the most was Marcantonio della Torre. He was a young doctor who taught anatomy at the University of Pavia. When Leonardo began to study anatomy, he sat in on Marcantonio's classes. Leonardo took notes and drew what he saw at Marcantonio's dissections. Sadly, Marcantonio died when he was only twenty-nine. Leonardo lost a great teacher and a good friend.

Let's meet some more Renaissance folks!

Leon Battista Alberti

Leon Battista Alberti was a famous architect who was much older than Leonardo. He was also a poet, musician, philosopher, sculptor, and writer.

When Leonardo went to Florence, he studied the ideas of Leon Battista Alberti. Alberti's thinking greatly influenced Leonardo, especially his ideas about art. Alberti wrote a book about painting. He said that all painters should know about mathematics, poetry, and history.

Like Leonardo, Alberti loved animals. He trained horses and even wrote a book about his favorite dog. Alberti was very athletic. There is a story that he once threw an apple all the way to the top of the Duomo. (That's longer than a football field!)

Michelangelo Buonarroti

Michelangelo was one of the world's greatest artists. He created incredible paintings, drawings, and sculptures. He was also a skilled architect. Michelangelo's most famous works are his statues and the painting on the ceiling of the Sistine Chapel in Rome.

Michelangelo was a young man when he met Leonardo. Leonardo was in his fifties. The two did not get along. Leonardo always had very good manners. Michelangelo was often short-tempered. There are several stories about Michelangelo's rudeness to Leonardo.

While Leonardo was working on the *Battle of Anghiari*, Michelangelo was also painting his own mural in the same room. Michelangelo never finished his painting, either. He went to Rome to complete another work.

Donato Bramante

Donato Bramante was a painter and architect. When Bramante met Leonardo, he was designing an addition to a church in Milan.

Like Leonardo, Bramante was a genius. He began as a painter, but architecture was his passion. He shared his love of building with Leonardo and taught him many techniques.

And like Leonardo, Bramante was a musician. He played the lute. He was a kind and gentle man. Leonardo always called him Donnino. Bramante's friends liked to tease him. They once wrote a funny poem about his greediness for pears.

Bramante designed an incredible church called St. Peter's Basilica in Rome. Many people think it is the most beautiful church in the world.

Raphael

Art experts say that the greatest artists of the Renaissance were Leonardo, Michelangelo, and Raphael. Raphael was the youngest of the three.

Raphael grew up surrounded by art. His father was a court painter, and he taught his son how to draw and paint. The boy was a natural artist and learned quickly.

By the time he was a teenager, Raphael was so talented that people began to call him a master. Everyone seemed to love the handsome, friendly boy.

Raphael was influenced by the works of Leonardo and Michelangelo. During his short life, he produced many incredible paintings. But at the height of his fame, Raphael caught a fever. He died in Rome on his thirty-seventh birthday. Thousands attended his funeral. His last painting rested at the head of his coffin.

7

Death of a Genius

Leonardo was getting old. His health was failing, and he had lost the use of his right hand. When Francis I, the king of France, asked him to come to France, Leonardo accepted. Francis offered him a country house near his palace. He and the king spent many hours together, talking about art and science.

Leonardo devoted his last three years to organizing his papers. He died in 1519, when he was sixty-seven years old. For years, many people believed that he died in Francis's arms. Experts now believe that Francis was away when Leonardo died.

Leonardo was buried in the Cathedral of Saint-Florentin in France. By 1802, the cathedral was in ruins. Builders used the gravestones to repair a nearby mansion. Today no one knows where Leonardo's body lies.

Leonardo's Notebooks

As late as 1966, two notebooks were found in the National Library of Spain.

Leonardo left his friends a few books and some paintings. Leonardo's beloved assistant, Francesco Melzi, took charge of the notebooks. After Melzi died, many pages of the notebooks were lost, sold, or stolen. Lots of people wanted pages from the genius's notebooks.

Leonardo's Gifts

As the years passed, people mainly remembered Leonardo as a painter. They forgot all the other things he did. Finally museums and libraries began to collect what remained of his notebooks. It took almost 400 years before people were able to study them seriously.

When this happened, people realized the full genius of Leonardo. They saw his gifts as a scientist and inventor. They read his thoughts about nature and art and architecture. And they saw that many of Leonardo's ideas were right.

Today Leonardo's work inspires people of all ages. He would be amazed to know that every year, eight million people go to the Louvre just to see his favorite painting, the *Mona Lisa*.

King Francis I said that there has never
been another man who knew as much as

Leonardo da Vinci. Many people feel that there will never be another like him.

Doing More Research

There's a lot more you can learn about Leonardo da Vinci and his world. The fun of research is seeing how many different sources you can explore.

Books

Most libraries and bookstores have lots of books about Leonardo.

Here are some things to remember when you're using books for research:

1. You don't have to read the whole book. Check the table of contents and the index to find the topics you're interested in.

2. Write down the name of the book.

When you take notes, make sure you write down the name of the book in your notebook so you can find it again.

3. Never copy exactly from a book.

When you learn something new from a book, put it in your own words.

4. Make sure the book is <u>nonfiction</u>.

Some books tell new, make-believe stories about Leonardo da Vinci. Make-believe stories are called *fiction*. They're fun to read, but not good for research.

Research books have facts and tell true stories. They are called *nonfiction*. A librarian or teacher can help you make sure the books you use for research are non-fiction.

Here are some good nonfiction books about Leonardo and the Renaissance:

- *Amazing Leonardo da Vinci Inventions You Can Build Yourself* by Maxine Anderson

- *Leonardo da Vinci* by Diane Stanley

- *Leonardo da Vinci for Kids: His Life and Ideas* by Janis Herbert

- *Leonardo da Vinci: The Genius Who Defined the Renaissance* by John Phillips

- *Michelangelo,* Getting to Know the World's Greatest Artists series, by Mike Venezia

- *Renaissance,* a DK Eyewitness Book, by Alison Cole

Museums

Many museums have permanent exhibits of Leonardo's work. Also, there are often traveling exhibits that may appear in museums in your area, so look around! These places can help you learn more about Leonardo da Vinci and his world.

When you go to a museum:

1. Be sure to take your notebook!
Write down anything that catches your interest. Draw pictures, too!

2. Ask questions.
There are almost always people at museums who can help you find what you're looking for.

3. Check the calendar.
Many museums have special events and activities just for kids!

109

Here are some museums with permanent Leonardo exhibits:

- J. Paul Getty Museum (Los Angeles)

- Metropolitan Museum of Art
  (New York)

- National Gallery of Art (Washington,
  D.C.)

DVDs

There are some great nonfiction DVDs about Leonardo da Vinci. As with books, make sure the DVDs you watch for research are nonfiction!

Check your library or video store for these and other nonfiction titles about Leonardo:

- *Leonardo da Vinci,* Getting to Know the World's Greatest Artists series
  created and directed by Mike Venezia

- *Leonardo da Vinci: Renaissance Master* from A&E Biography

- *Leonardo da Vinci,* The Animated Hero Classics series
  from Nest Family Learning

- *Leonardo's Dream Machines* from PBS

The Internet

Many websites have facts about Leonardo and the Renaissance. Some also have games and activities that can help make learning about Leonardo even more fun.

Ask your teacher or your parents to help you find more websites like these:

- bbc.co.uk/science/leonardo

- cybersleuthkids.com/sleuth/Science /Inventors/Leonardo_Da_Vinci/index.htm

- enchantedlearning.com/inventors/page/d /davinci.shtml

- mos.org/leonardo

Good luck!

Index

*Have you read the adventure that
matches up with this book?*

Don't miss

Magic Tree House® Merlin Mission #10

MONDAY WITH A MAD GENIUS

The magic tree house whisks Jack and Annie
to Italy in the Renaissance, a time when every
new morning brought with it the promise of
artistic and scientific wonder. There, they meet
none other than Leonardo da Vinci!

Enough cool facts
to fill a tree house!

Jack and Annie have been all over the world in their adventures in the magic tree house. And they've learned lots of incredible facts along the way. Now they want to share them with you! Get ready for a collection of the weirdest, grossest, funniest, most all-around amazing facts that Jack and Annie have ever encountered. It's the ultimate fact attack!

YOU'LL LOVE FINDING OUT THE FACTS BEHIND THE FICTION IN

Magic Tree House® Fact Tracker

Ghosts

A NONFICTION COMPANION TO MAGIC TREE HOUSE® MERLIN MISSION #14:
A Good Night for Ghosts

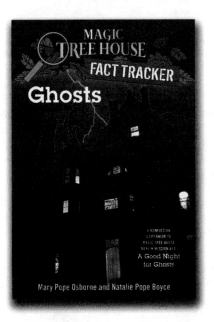

It's Jack and Annie's very own guide
to the stories about ghosts!

Available now!

Magic Tree House®

Magic Tree House® Merlin Missions

Magic Tree House® Super Edition

#1: WORLD AT WAR, 1944

Magic Tree House® Fact Trackers

DINOSAURS
KNIGHTS AND CASTLES
MUMMIES AND PYRAMIDS
PIRATES
RAIN FORESTS
SPACE
TITANIC
TWISTERS AND OTHER TERRIBLE STORMS
DOLPHINS AND SHARKS
ANCIENT GREECE AND THE OLYMPICS
AMERICAN REVOLUTION
SABERTOOTHS AND THE ICE AGE
PILGRIMS
ANCIENT ROME AND POMPEII
TSUNAMIS AND OTHER NATURAL DISASTERS
POLAR BEARS AND THE ARCTIC
SEA MONSTERS
PENGUINS AND ANTARCTICA
LEONARDO DA VINCI
GHOSTS
LEPRECHAUNS AND IRISH FOLKLORE
RAGS AND RICHES: KIDS IN THE TIME OF
    CHARLES DICKENS
SNAKES AND OTHER REPTILES
DOG HEROES
ABRAHAM LINCOLN

PANDAS AND OTHER ENDANGERED SPECIES
HORSE HEROES
HEROES FOR ALL TIMES
SOCCER
NINJAS AND SAMURAI
CHINA: LAND OF THE EMPEROR'S GREAT
    WALL
SHARKS AND OTHER PREDATORS
VIKINGS
DOGSLEDDING AND EXTREME SPORTS
DRAGONS AND MYTHICAL CREATURES
WORLD WAR II

More Magic Tree House®

GAMES AND PUZZLES FROM THE TREE HOUSE
MAGIC TRICKS FROM THE TREE HOUSE
MY MAGIC TREE HOUSE JOURNAL
MAGIC TREE HOUSE SURVIVAL GUIDE
ANIMAL GAMES AND PUZZLES
MAGIC TREE HOUSE INCREDIBLE FACT BOOK

CALLING ALL ADVENTURERS!
Join the
MAGIC TREE HOUSE®
KIDS' ADVENTURE CLUB
Members receive:
• Exclusive packages delivered throughout the year
• Members-only swag
• A sneak peek at upcoming books
• Access to printables, games, giveaways, and more!
With a parent's help, visit MagicTreeHouse.com to learn more and to sign up!
© 2016 Mary Pope Osborne. Magic Tree House is a registered trademark of Mary Pope Osborne; used under license. Illustrations © 2016 by Sal Murdocca.
RHCB
MagicTreeHouse.com

BRING MAGIC TREE HOUSE TO YOUR SCHOOL!

Magic Tree House musicals now available for performance by young people!

Ask your teacher or director to contact Music Theatre International for more information:
BroadwayJr.com
Licensing@MTIshows.com
(212) 541-4684

MAGIC TREE HOUSE COLLECTION
DINOSAURS BEFORE DARK KIDS

MAGIC TREE HOUSE COLLECTION
The Knight at Dawn KIDS

ATTENTION, TEACHERS!

Mary Pope Osborne's Classroom Adventures Program

The Magic Tree House **CLASSROOM ADVENTURES PROGRAM** is a free, comprehensive set of online educational resources for teachers developed by Mary Pope Osborne as a gift to teachers, to thank them for their enthusiastic support of the series. Educators can learn more at MTHClassroomAdventures.org.

MAGIC TREE HOUSE